My Path to Math

123456789

USING A CALCULATOR

Marsha Arvoy and
Dorianne Nardi

Crabtree Publishing Company

www.crabtreebooks.com

Author: Marsha Arvoy and Dorianne Nardi
Publishing plan research and development:
  Sean Charlebois, Reagan Miller
  Crabtree Publishing Company
Editor: Molly Aloian
Editorial director: Kathy Middleton
Project coordinator: Margaret Salter
Prepress technician: Margaret Salter
Coordinating editor: Chester Fisher
Series editor: Jessica Cohn
Project manager: Kumar Kunal (Q2AMEDIA)
Art direction: Dibakar Acharjee (Q2AMEDIA)
Cover design: Shruti Aggarwal (Q2AMEDIA)
Design: Shruti Aggarwal (Q2AMEDIA)
Photo research: Poulomi Basu (Q2AMEDIA)

Photographs:
Shutterstock: Juliengrondin/Szocs Jozsef/Tania Zbrodko: front cover, folio image, icon image; Sergei Telegin: title page; Photomak: p. 4 (top); Yuri Shirokov: p. 4 (bottom); Ilker Canikligil: p. 9; J. Helgason: p. 11; Nassyrov Ruslan: p. 15, 23; Iofoto: p. 19 (top, right); Dmitriy Shironosov: p. 19 (top, left); Yuri Arcurs: p. 19 (top, middle), Juliengrondin: folio, icon
Big Stock Photo: Kae Horng Mau: p. 17, p. 19 (bottom, right)
Dreamstime: Jonathan Ross: p. 7
Istockphoto: Jennifer Borton: p. 6; Lovely Hart Photography: p. 12
Judy Glick Smith: p. 5, p. 13, p. 19 (bottom, left), p. 21
Masterfile: Scanpix Creative: p. 8
Comstock: p. 20

Q2AMedia Art Bank: p. 11

Library and Archives Canada Cataloguing in Publication

Arvoy, Marsha
    Using a calculator / Marsha Arvoy & Dorianne Nardi.

(My path to math)
Includes index.
ISBN 978-0-7787-5252-3 (bound).--ISBN 978-0-7787-5299-8 (pbk.)

    1. Calculators--Juvenile literature. I. Nardi, Dorianne II. Title.
III. Series: My path to math

QA75.A78 2009   j510.28'4   C2009-905364-0

Library of Congress Cataloging-in-Publication Data

Arvoy, Marsha.
  Using a calculator / Marsha Arvoy & Dorianne Nardi.
    p. cm. -- (My path to math)
  Includes index.
  ISBN 978-0-7787-5252-3 (reinforced lib. bdg. : alk. paper) -- ISBN 978-0-7787-5299-8 (pbk. : alk. paper)
  1. Calculators--Juvenile literature. I. Nardi, Dorianne. II. Title. III. Series.

  QA75.A768 2010
  510.28'4--dc22

                2009035499

Crabtree Publishing Company

www.crabtreebooks.com   1-800-387-7650

Printed in China/122009/CT20090903

Published in Canada
Crabtree Publishing
616 Welland Ave.
St. Catharines, ON
L2M 5V6

Published in the United States
Crabtree Publishing
PMB 59051
350 Fifth Avenue, 59th Floor
New York, New York 10118

Published in the United Kingdom
Crabtree Publishing
Maritime House
Basin Road North, Hove
BN41 1WR

Published in Australia
Crabtree Publishing
386 Mt. Alexander Rd.
Ascot Vale (Melbourne)
VIC 3032

Contents

The Gift of Math

Ann's family is having a reunion! Her grandfather is staying at her house. He has brought her a special present. It is a **calculator**. He knows that she likes math.

A calculator is a tool that people use to help them **solve** math problems.

Activity Box

Can you think of a time when you used a calculator?

Ann was hoping to get
a calculator of her own.

Using a Calculator

Grandfather tells Ann that a calculator is used to solve problems with large numbers. It is also used to solve problems with many different numbers.

You can use a calculator to check answers, too. First, you solve the problem on paper or in your head. It is best to use your brain first! Then check the answer with your calculator.

Activity Box

Look at this problem: 4 + 1 = __
Would you use a calculator to solve this problem?
Why or why not?

The more you solve problems on paper, the faster you can solve them in your head.

Parts and Functions

Ann sees a little screen on the calculator. She also sees buttons with numbers and **symbols**. Ann's grandfather tells her about each button and its **function**.

He points to the on/off button. She pushes it, and the screen shows the number 0. The calculator is on.

She finds the
addition (+) button.
She looks for the
division (÷) button, too.

Activity Box

What do you see on your calculator? Can you find the button that means to **multiply**?

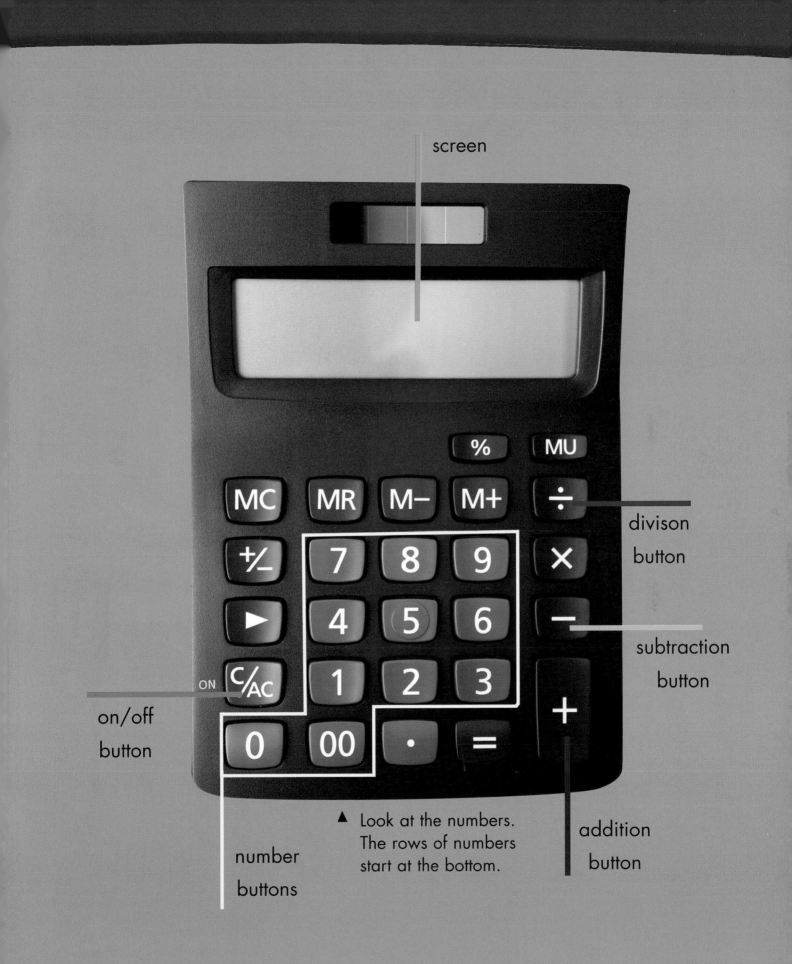

screen

% MU

MC MR M− M+ ÷

divison
button

+/− 7 8 9 ×

▶ 4 5 6 −

subtraction
button

ON C/AC 1 2 3

on/off
button

0 00 · = +

▲ Look at the numbers.
The rows of numbers
start at the bottom.

number
buttons

addition
button

Addition

Ann's dad brings home balloons for the reunion. Ann sees five yellow balloons, seven red balloons, and eight green balloons. She wants to know how many balloons there are in all.

Ann uses a pencil and paper to solve this problem. She draws a picture of all the balloons and then adds them up. Then she checks her answer using the calculator.

$$5 \ + \ 7 \ + \ 8 \ = \ 20$$

She sees that the answer is 20. She was correct!

Activity Box

Try solving this problem using paper and a pencil. Then check your answer using a calculator. There are 4 yellow balloons, 3 red balloons, and 2 green balloons. How many are there altogether?

$+$ $+$

$= $ **2O**

When you want to know the
answer, you press the button
with the "equal"sign.

equal sign button

Subtraction

It is time to get food ready for the party. Ann places cheese on a plate with 24 crackers. Her dad and grandfather eat a total of nine crackers! She wonders how many are left. Ann counts backward from 24 in her head.

23... 22... 21... 20... 19... 18... 17... 16... 15!

Ann's grandfather tells her that the calculator can check her answer. Ann presses the following buttons to check.

24 – 9 =15

The number 15 shows up on the screen. She was right again.

Activity Box

Imagine that there are 36 crackers. Your family eats 11. Count backward from 36 in your head. Count back 11. Then check your answer with a calculator. 36 - 11 = ⸺

12

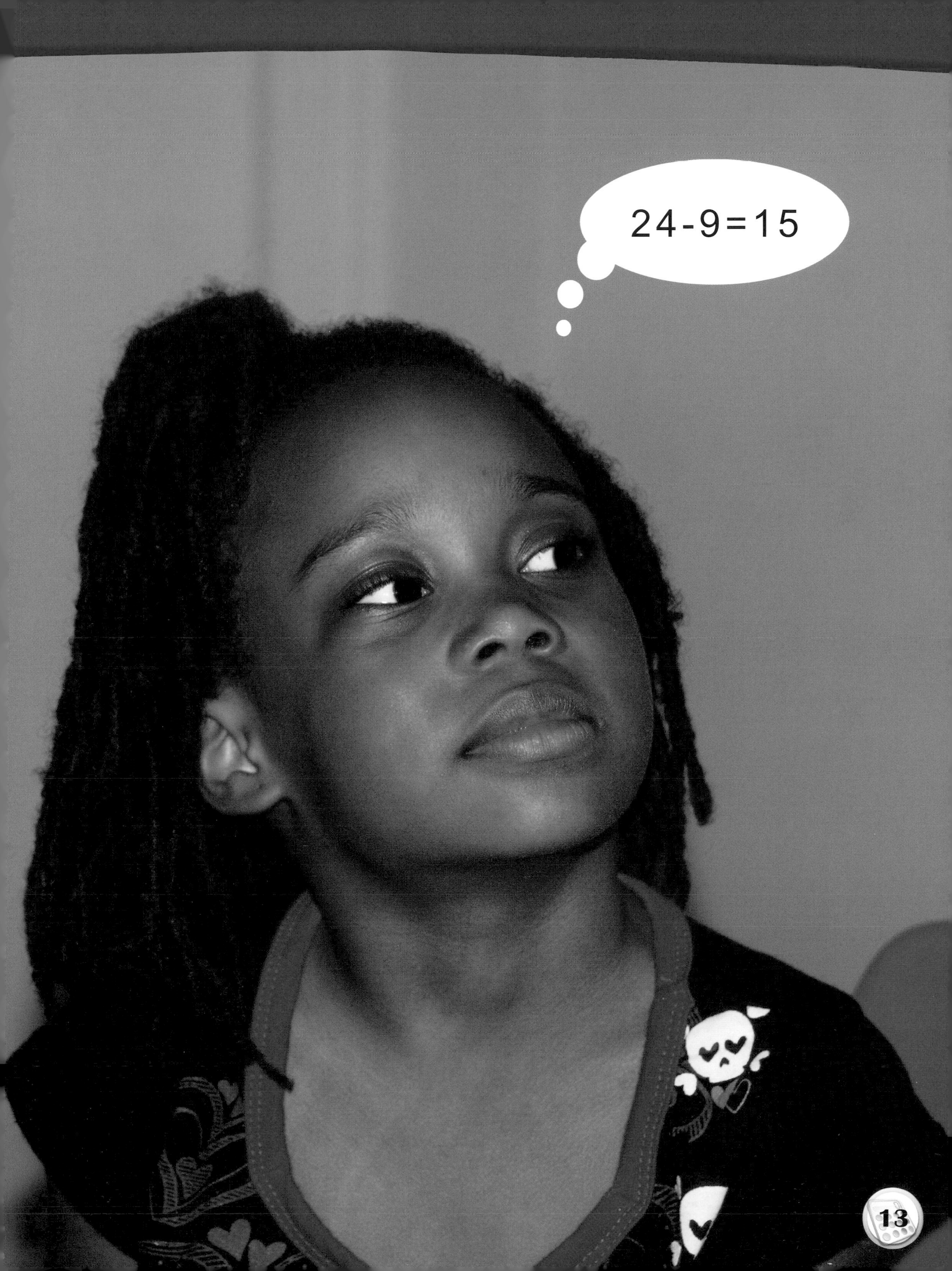
24-9=15

Exploring Patterns

Ann's dad shows her how to see number **patterns** using a calculator. Looking at the numbers is like a game.

He asks Ann to choose a number. Ann chooses the number 4 and presses it on the calculator. Next he tells her to add 1 then press the equal sign. Ann sees that the answer is 5.

4   +   1   =   5

He tells her to press the equal sign again and again. The number on the calculator keeps changing.

6... 7... 8... 9... 10!

Each time she presses the equal sign, the total increases by 1. The pattern is adding 1.

There are things to count, add, and subtract all around you!

Activity Box

Try adding these numbers. Press the equal button five times, as Ann did. What patterns do you notice?

2 + 2 =   5 + 5 =   10 + 10 =

Estimation

Ann has a three-year-old dog named Fluffy. Her mom says that every year in a person's life is like seven years in a dog's life. "What is Fluffy's age in dog years?" she asks Ann.

Ann uses the information she knows to make an **estimate**. She knows that 5 added together three times is 15. Since 7 is larger than 5, she knows that the answer must be more than 15. She estimates that Fluffy is about 20 years old in dog years. Then she checks her estimate on the calculator. Fluffy is three years old. So Ann adds 7 three times, once for every year.

7   +   7   +   7   =

Fluffy is 21 years old!

Ann's estimate of Fluffy's age is very close to the right answer!

Activity Box

Estimate how old a five-year-old dog would be in dog years. Check your answer with a calculator. How close was your answer?

Fun Calculations

Ann's grandfather says that adding 7 three times together is the same as multiplying 7 times 3. Ann tries the multiplication problem on the calculator.

7   x   3   =   21

Fluffy truly is 21 in dog years! Ann then takes a **survey** to find out the ages of the people in her family.

Name	Dad	Grandfather	Ann	Mom
Age	42	63	7	40

Fluffy is older than Ann but younger than the rest of her family—at least, in dog years!

Activity Box

Can you think of a fun way to use your calculator? Share your idea with a friend.

Multiplication is fun when you get the hang of it.

Getting Answers

Ann likes her new calculator. She knows she can use it for many different activities. She can solve problems, check her answers, find patterns, and have fun.

Next, Ann tries division on the calculator. Ann helped her Mom make 28 sandwiches. There are 14 guests at the reunion. How many sandwiches are there for each guest? Ann can find the answer if she divides the number of sandwiches by the number of guests.

28 ÷ 14 = 2

There are 2 sandwiches for each guest.

Look in the glossary and index to think about the kinds of problems a calculator can help you solve.

Glossary

addition Combination of two or more amounts to make a bigger amount

calculator Tool used to help solve math problems

division Math operation in which a number is cut into equal parts

estimate An educated guess or to make an educated guess

function What something does

multiply To increase the amount or number of something; to add an amount to itself a certain number of times

patterns Things that are repeated

solve To find an answer

survey Collection of information

symbols Signs that represent something else

Index